Awesome
ABYSSINIANS

ACTIVE! SMART! FRIENDLY!

LONG! SLIM! MUSCULAR!

ABDO
Publishing Company

Anders Hanson

Consulting Editor, Diane Craig, M.A./Reading Specialist

Published by ABDO Publishing Company
8000 West 78th Street, Edina, Minnesota 55439.

Printed in the United States.

 PRINTED ON RECYCLED PAPER

Editor: Liz Salzmann
Content Developer: Nancy Tuminelly
Cover and Interior Design and Production:
    Anders Hanson, Mighty Media
Illustrations: Bob Doucet
Photo Credits: Shutterstock

Library of Congress Cataloging-in-Publication Data
Hanson, Anders, 1980-
  Awesome abyssinians / Anders Hanson ; illustrations by
Bob Doucet.
    p. cm. -- (Cat craze)
  ISBN 978-1-60453-721-5
  1. Abyssinian cat--Juvenile literature. I. Doucet, Bob, ill. II.
Title.

 SF449.A28H36 2010
 636.8'26--dc22
                    2009003038

Super SandCastle™ books are created by a team of
professional educators, reading specialists, and content
developers around five essential components—phonemic
awareness, phonics, vocabulary, text comprehension, and
fluency—to assist young readers as they develop reading
skills and strategies and increase their general
knowledge. All books are written, reviewed, and leveled
for guided reading, early reading intervention, and
Accelerated Reader® programs for use in shared, guided,
and independent reading and writing activities to support
a balanced approach to literacy instruction.

CONTENTS

The
ABYSSINIAN

Abyssinians are intelligent, playful cats. They are very friendly, but most Abyssinians do not like to be cuddled.

Abyssinians are medium-sized cats. They are slender and **muscular**.

Abyssinian cats are sometimes called Abys.

FACIAL FEATURES

Head

An Abyssinian's head is shaped like a rounded, upside-down triangle.

Muzzle

An Abyssinian has a rounded **muzzle**.

Eyes

Abyssinians have large, almond-shaped eyes. They are usually amber or green.

Ears

Abyssinians have large ears that are set far apart.

BODY BASICS

Size

Adult Abyssinians weigh about 7 to 12 pounds (3 to 5 kg).

Build

Abyssinians have slender, **muscular** builds.

Tail

Abyssinians have long tails. They are thick at the base and narrow at the tip.

Legs and Feet

Abyssinians have slender legs with oval feet.

COAT & COLOR

Abyssinian Fur

Abyssinian cats have short, thick coats. Their fur is soft and shiny.

Abys have ticked fur. This means that each hair has bands of light and dark color. This gives the coat a **speckled**, sandy look.

Abyssinian cats come in several colors. The four most common colors are ruddy, red, fawn, and blue.

Ruddy coats are brown with dark brown or black ticking. Red Abys are a deep red color with brown ticking. Fawn coats are tan with light brown ticking. Blue Abyssinians have a tan coat with dark, blue-gray ticking.

RUDDY FUR

RUDDY ADULT

RED FUR

FAWN FUR

BLUE FUR

RED ADULT

FAWN KITTEN

BLUE ADULT

HEALTH & CARE

Life Span

Most Abyssinians live to be 10 to 12 years old.

Health Concerns

As a **breed**, Abyssinians are quite healthy. However, a few Abyssinians get a **kidney disease** called renal amyloidosis. This disease can lead to kidney failure.

VET'S CHECKLIST

- Have your Abyssinian spayed or neutered. This will prevent unwanted kittens.

- Visit a vet for regular checkups.

- Ask your vet which foods are right for your Abyssinian.

- Brush your Abyssinian's teeth every day.

- Ask your vet about shots that may benefit your cat.

ATTITUDE & BEHAVIOR

Personality

Abyssinians are friendly and playful. They love to be around people they know. Abyssinians are curious, intelligent cats. They may even figure out how to open doors and drawers.

Activity Level

Abyssinians are very active cats. They love to run. They also enjoy climbing tall objects. Most Abys would rather play or explore than sit quietly on your lap.

All About Me

Hi! My name is Abby. I'm an Abyssinian. I just wanted to let you know a few things about me. I made some lists below of things I like and dislike. Check them out!

Things I Like

- Climbing tall objects or furniture
- Being around my family
- Small children
- Opening drawers and doors
- Playing with toys
- Exploring my surroundings
- Being active
- Playing with water

Things I Dislike

- Being picked up or cuddled
- Being kept in small spaces
- Strangers
- Not being included in my family's activities

LITTERS & KITTENS

Litter Size

Female Abyssinians usually give birth to three to five kittens.

Diet

Newborn kittens drink their mother's milk. They can begin to eat kitten food when they are about six weeks old. Kitten food is different from cat food. It has extra **protein**, fat, and **vitamins** that help kittens grow.

Growth

Abyssinian kittens should stay with their mothers for two to three months. An Abyssinian will be almost full grown when it is six months old. But it will continue to grow slowly until it is one year old.

BUYING AN ABYSSINIAN

Choosing a Breeder

It's best to buy a kitten from a **breeder**, not a pet store. When you visit a cat breeder, ask to see the mother and father of the kittens. Make sure the parents are healthy, friendly, and well behaved.

Picking a Kitten

Choose a kitten that isn't too active or too shy. If you sit down, some of the kittens may come over to you. One of them might be the right one for you!

Is It the Right Cat for You?

Buying a cat is a big decision. You'll want to make sure your new pet suits your lifestyle.

Get out a piece of paper. Draw a line down the middle.

Read the statements listed here. Each time you agree with a statement from the left column, make a mark on the left side of your paper. When you agree with a statement from the right column, make a mark on the right side of your paper.

I want a cat that loves spending time with me.	☐ ☐	I want a cat that stays out of my business.
I don't need to cuddle with my cat.	☐ ☐	I want a lap cat.
I want a playful, energetic cat.	☐ ☐	I like lazy cats.
I live in a large apartment or house.	☐ ☐	I live in a small apartment.
I want a smart cat.	☐ ☐	I don't want a cat that can open doors and drawers.

If you made more marks on the left side than on the right side, an Abyssinian may be the right cat for you! If you made more marks on the right side of your paper, you might want to consider another breed.

Some Things You'll Need

Cats go to the bathroom in a **litter box**. It should be kept in a quiet place. Most cats learn to use their litter box all by themselves. You just have to show them where it is! The dirty **litter** should be scooped out every day. The litter should be changed completely every week.

Your cat's **food and water dishes** should be wide and shallow. This helps your cat keep its whiskers clean. The dishes should be in a different area than the litter box. Cats do not like to eat and go to the bathroom in the same area.

Cats love to scratch! **Scratching posts** help keep cats from scratching the furniture. The scratching post should be taller than your cat. It should have a wide, heavy base so it won't tip over.

Cats are natural predators. Without small animals to hunt, cats may become bored and unhappy. **Cat toys** can satisfy your cat's need to chase and capture. They will help keep your cat entertained and happy.

Cats should not play with balls of yarn or string. If they accidentally eat the yarn, they could get sick.

Cat claws should be trimmed regularly with special cat claw **clippers**. Regular nail clippers will also work. Some people choose to have their cat's claws removed by a vet. But most vets and animal rights groups think declawing is cruel.

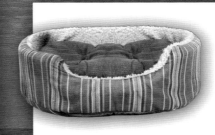

You should brush your cat regularly with a **cat hair brush**. This will help keep its coat healthy and clean.

A **cat bed** will give your cat a safe, comfortable place to sleep.

LIVING WITH AN ABYSSINIAN

Being a Good Companion

Abyssinians need a lot of attention. They love to be around people. They enjoy being included in many of their family's activities. However, most Abyssinians don't like to be cuddled or picked up.

Inside or Outside?

Abyssinians are active cats. They need space to run and play. They may feel uncomfortable in small apartments.

Most vets say that it is best for cats to be kept inside. That way the cats are safe from predators and cars.

Feeding Your Abyssinian

Abyssinians may be fed regular cat food. They are more energetic than most cats. They need to eat a little more than less active cats do.

Cleaning the Litter Box

Like all cats, Abyssinians are tidy. They don't like smelly or dirty litter boxes. If the litter box is dirty, they may go to the bathroom somewhere else. Ask your vet for advice if your cat isn't using its box.

DANGER: POISONOUS FOODS

Some people like to feed their cats table scraps. Here are some human foods that can make cats sick.

TOMATOES

POTATOES

ONIONS

GARLIC

CHOCOLATE

GRAPES

THE ANCIENT ABYSSINIAN

The history of the Abyssinian **breed** is uncertain. Some people believe that Abyssinian cats are **descendants** of ancient Egyptian cats.

The ancient Egyptians **worshipped** many gods. One of their gods was a cat called Bastet. Bastet was the goddess of protection and motherhood.

Abyssinians do look very much like the cats in ancient Egyptian art. But there are no facts to prove that the two **breeds** are directly connected. Some scientists believe Abyssinians are **descendants** of wild cats from southeast Asia.

FIND THE ABYSSINIAN

A

B

C

D

THE ABYSSINIAN QUIZ

1. Abyssinians are medium-sized cats. **True or false?**

2. Abyssinians have small ears. **True or false?**

3. Abyssinian cats have long, shaggy coats. **True or false?**

4. Abyssinians are active cats. **True or false?**

5. Abyssinians like being picked up. **True or false?**

6. Abyssinians look like cats seen in ancient Egyptian art. **True or false?**

GLOSSARY

breed – a group of animals or plants with common ancestors. A *breeder* is someone whose job is to breed certain animals or plants.

descendant – a person or animal that is related to an older person or animal.

disease – a sickness.

kidney – the organ in the body that turns waste from the blood into urine.

muscular – having a lot of strong muscles.

muzzle – an animal's nose and jaws.

protein – a substance found in all plant and animal cells.

speckled – having a lot of small spots of color.

vitamin – a substance needed for good health, found naturally in plants and meats.

worship – to honor or respect as a god or supernatural power.

About SUPER SANDCASTLE™

Bigger Books for Emerging Readers
Grades K–4

Created for library, classroom, and at-home use, Super SandCastle™ books support and engage young readers as they develop and build literacy skills and will increase their general knowledge about the world around them. Super SandCastle™ books are part of SandCastle™, the leading preK–3 imprint for emerging and beginning readers. Super SandCastle™ features a larger trim size for more reading fun.

Let Us Know

Super SandCastle™ would like to hear your stories about reading this book. What was your favorite page? Was there something hard that you needed help with? Share the ups and downs of learning to read. We want to hear from you! Send us an e-mail.

sandcastle@abdopublishing.com

Contact us for a complete list of SandCastle™, Super SandCastle™, and other nonfiction and fiction titles from ABDO Publishing Company.

www.abdopublishing.com • 8000 West 78th Street Edina, MN 55439 • 800-800-1312 • 952-831-1632 fax